Poem of the Deep Song

POEMA DEL CANTE JONDO

POEM OF THE DEEP SONG

FEDERICO GARCÍA LORCA

TRANSLATED BY RALPH ANGEL

Sarabande Books

LOUISVILLE, KENTUCKY

FIRST EDITION

Managing Editor
Sarabande Books, Inc.
2234 Dundee Road, Suite 200
Louisville, KY 40205

Library of Congress Cataloging-in-Publication Data

García Lorca, Federico, 1898-1936.
    [Poema del cante jondo. English & Spanish]
    Poema del cante jondo = Poem of the deep song / Federico García Lorca ; translated by Ralph Angel.— 1st ed.
      p.   cm.
    ISBN 1-932511-40-7 (pbk. : alk. paper)
    I. Title: Poem of the deep song. II. Angel, Ralph, 1951- III. Title.
    PQ6613.A763P613 2006
    861'.62—dc22   2006004476

ISBN 13: 978-1-932511-40-6

Cover image provided by Herederos de Federico García Lorca

Cover and text design by Charles Casey Martin

Manufactured in the United States of America.
This book is printed on acid-free paper.

Sarabande Books is a nonprofit literary organization.

THE KENTUCKY ARTS COUNCIL

The Kentucky Arts Council, a state agency in the Commerce Cabinet, provides operational support funding for Sarabande Books with state tax dollars and federal funding from the National Endowment for the Arts, which believes that a great nation deserves great art.

CONTENTS

INTRODUCTION

The Black Torso of the Pharaoh

". . . articulate shivers, akin to instrumentation."
—Mallarmé

When Federico García Lorca met the Andalusian *cantaor* Manuel Torre in 1927, he overheard the famous singer reveal one pathway to the hidden caves of *duende*: "What you must search for and find," Torre said, "is the black torso of the Pharaoh." This revelation, which subtly refers to the popular theory that the Gypsy tribes of Europe descended from the Egyptians, must have intrigued and thrilled the poet. Lorca longed to find conclusive evidence of Gypsy blood in his own lineage, to justify his preternatural interest in Gypsy language and lore as sources of his own poetic capabilities. And as the end of the decade approached, he was on the cusp of an all-consuming infatuation with the mysteries of death, brought to the forefront of his obsessions by his complex, stimulating relationship with the Catalonian painter, Salvador Dalí. I think it was perhaps at this point in time, having just given *Romancero gitano* (Revista de Occidente, Madrid, 1928) to a prestigious publisher, and beginning to feel the pressures of becoming a well-known poet in Spain, that Lorca began to rekindle his own affection for the manuscript of *Poema del cante jondo* (Ediciones Ulises, Madrid, 1931).

Any man, woman, or child introduced to García Lorca in Madrid or Granada in 1921, while he was composing *Poem of the Deep Song*, would have found him to be a well-dressed, slender young man with olive skin, an unruly shock of jet-black hair, and dark, expressive eyes. His personality was a combination of playfulness and intensity, shot through with relentless curiosity about everything. He loved spontaneity and gatherings

ix

of friends and family. He was surprisingly religious in a spiritual rather than a doctrinal way; he enjoyed High Mass as a spectacle, especially the music. He was both fearful of and fascinated by physical violence and the concept of eternal damnation, but in his capable hands the piano became an instrument of natural and serious joy.

What might not have been apparent in 1921 was that Lorca was in the shallows of what was to be an extraordinarily sustained implosion of poetic activity that would last for more than a decade. He had just simultaneously begun another book of poems that would be written in long sequences, and eventually published as *Suites* (Ariel, Barcelona, 1983). A few of these lyrics were so completely hermetic they might have collapsed in on themselves like windless sails if not for the fact that the poet's persona was wide enough to absorb and reflect in silver moonlight the geographical and mythical landscape of Andalusia in its entirety.

It certainly is a rare gift for a poet to have a constant stream of visual, historical, mythical, and sensual subject matter passing by the window. In an essay he wrote to introduce the concept of a festival in Granada celebrating *cante jondo*, Lorca described what he perceived to be the emotional schematic of a typical evening in old Granada: "the blue remoteness of the vega, the Sierra greeting the tremulous Mediterranean, the enormous barbs of the clouds, sunk into the distance, the admirable rubato of the city. . . ." This is an ancient list. Its elements existed before language was invented, and it is one of the ambient keys with which Lorca unlocked the unwritten mystery of the music he would follow unerringly to find his own *duende*.

In the tenth century, after nearly 300 years of Saracen and Moorish rule, Andalusia had become the caliphate of Córdoba, and one of Europe's most populous and prosperous areas. It was the seat of Islamic political life, and of its literary and artistic

culture. But for much of its history, Andalusia had also been magnetic for conflicting waves of immigrants: Romans, Goths, Jews, Visigoths, Gypsies, and finally the Moors.

The apex of Moorish culture, which is represented for eternity by the Alhambra in Granada, was hollowed out from below by the brutal, secular incursions of the crusaders, and brought to an abrupt end during the reconquest of Andalusia by the Castilian army of King Ferdinand and Queen Isabella. In 1492, the famed forests of Moguer provided the sturdy planks for the ships of Columbus, which were manned by Andalusian sailors and launched toward the Americas from the Andalusian port of Palos. But by the time of the destruction of the Spanish Armada off the coasts of England and Ireland in 1588, Andalusia had splintered into several distinct cities, each with its own character, and soon it, too, sank like a breached caravel from the sight of the world. It was at that bleak point in its chronology, I'm convinced, that Andalusia's Gypsy *cantaores*, if indeed there were any then, began to be called upon for the consolation inherent in their art.

Deep song is nothing if it does not companion the night, no matter how long the darkness might last. "We are a sad, static people," Lorca wrote of his fellow Andalusians, "people [who] cross their arms in prayer, look at the stars, and wait uselessly for a sign of salvation." But it is one of the truths of the earth, it seems to me, that those who can find stillness in the face of sorrow and turmoil are often those in whom great revelations are instilled. "Static," Lorca's description of the Andalusians, is a word that also invokes the idea of the power of the force of life, potential energy waiting to be called upon by those who must have it to survive.

Duende, born of the mystery and power of death, nevertheless has everything to do with life on the earth. In order to make itself heard and felt, *duende* must pass through a living

body, the voices of the *cantaores*, and the recitations of the poets. In one of his essays on deep song, Lorca recalls the words of an ancient guitar player who told him that *duende* pressed up through the crust of the earth and into him through the soles of his feet. The power of *duende*, like the mystical power of the Pharaohs, is from something majestic like the pyramids, and when it has made itself heard, it passes back into its secret subterranean chambers, far from view.

Before his premature departure from the world, Lorca went down into the caves of *duende* many times. He listened with intensity and wrote down the music that he heard, for those who would follow him on his way, or who could not hear the music at all. In Spain, where unrest had been festering beneath the surface since the Inquisition against the Jews and other non-Catholic believers, and the expulsion by Royal Decree of the *moriscos* in 1609, up to the twentieth-century anarchists whose exploits filled the newspapers of Lorca's time, there was soon going to be plenty of death to go around, including the poet's own murder in 1936. But no matter how rudely he might have been thrust into the dusty ground beneath impassive olive trees, no matter how painful and senseless the loss of his life still seems to those who revere his poetic accomplishments, Lorca has been reunited with his precious black Pharaoh.

Luckily for all of us, many of the images, intimations, and signs that Lorca left behind wait patiently here in the pages of this book. They are remarkably intact and moving, considering the great age of the subject matter, presented in the powerful language of translation by Ralph Angel, another poet who cannot stop listening. He has revealed the many incidental felicities of Lorca's lyrics in a sensitive and seductive way, and called forth an unforgettable, bone-chilling evocation of the poet's timeless Andalusian voice.

Federico García Lorca . . . Blue archer whose quiver is never empty. . . *Te encuentras aquí mismo.*

— Greg Simon
Portland, Oregon

All quotations from Lorca's prose were taken from the marvelous book *Deep Song and Other Prose* (New Directions, New York, 1980), edited and translated by Christopher Maurer. His translations of the essays "Deep Song" and "Play and Theory of the Duende" also form the basis of a subsequent volume, *In Search of Duende* (New Directions, New York, 1998).

Poem of the Deep Song

POEMA DEL CANTE JONDO

Baladilla de los tres ríos

A Salvador Quintero

El río Guadalquivir
va entre naranjos y olivos.
Los dos ríos de Granada
bajan de la nieve al trigo.

¡Ay, amor,
que se fue y no vino!

El río Guadalquivir
tiene las barbas granates.
Los dos ríos de Granada
uno llanto y otro sangre.

¡Ay, amor,
que se fue por el aire! .

Para los barcos de vela,
Sevilla tiene un camino;
por el agua de Granada
sólo reman los suspiros.

¡Ay, amor,
que se fue y no vino!

Guadalquivir, alta torre
y viento en los naranjales.
Dauro y Genil, torrecillas
muertas sobre los estanques.

Ballad of Three Rivers

For Salvador Quintero

The river Guadalquivir
winds among orange trees and olive trees.
The two rivers of Granada
descend from the snow to the wheat.

Ay, love
that vanished and never returned!

The river Guadalquivir,
of garnet whiskers.
The two rivers of Granada,
one of tears, the other of blood.

Ay, love
that vanished into thin air!

For sailing ships
Sevilla's a safe passage;
in the waters of Granada
only sighs move about.

Ay, love
that vanished and never returned!

Guadalquivir, tall tower
and wind in the orange groves.
Dauro and Genil, deathly still towers
in the reflecting pools.

¡Ay, amor,
que se fue por el aire!

¡Quién dirá que el agua lleva
un fuego fatuo de gritos!

¡Ay, amor,
que se fue y no vino!

Lleva azahar, lleva olivas,
Andalucía, a tus mares.

¡Ay, amor,
que se fue por el aire!

Ay, love
that vanished into thin air!

One could say the water carries with it
a will-o'-the-wisp full of cries!

Ay, love
that vanished and never returned!

It carries olives and orange blossom,
Andalucía, down to your seas.

Ay, love
that vanished into thin air!

Poema de la Siguiriya gitana

A Carlos Morla Vicuña

PAISAJE

El campo
de olivos
se abre y se cierra
como un abanico.
Sobre el olivar
hay un cielo hundido
y una lluvia oscura
de luceros fríos.
Tiembla junco y penumbra
a la orilla del río.
Se riza el aire gris.
Los olivos
están cargados
de gritos.
Una bandada
de pájaros cautivos,
que mueven sus larguísimas
colas en lo sombrío.

Poem of the Gypsy Siguiriya

For Carlos Morla Vicuña

LANDSCAPE

The field
of olive trees
opens and closes
like a fan.
Above the groves
there is a low sky
and a dark shower
of cold, bright stars.
Reeds and twilight tremble
at the edge of the river.
The gray air spools.
The olive trees
are charged
with cries.
A flock
of captive birds,
their long, long tail feathers
fluttering in the gloom.

La guitarra

Empieza el llanto
de la guitarra.
Se rompen las copas
de la madrugada.
Empieza el llanto
de la guitarra.
Es inútil
callarla.
Es imposible
callarla.
Llora monótona
como llora el agua,
como llora el viento
sobre la nevada.
Es imposible
callarla.
Llora por cosas
lejanas.
Arena del Sur caliente
que pide camelias blancas.
Llora flecha sin blanco,
la tarde sin mañana,
y el primer pájaro muerto
sobre la rama.
¡Oh guitarra!
Corazón malherido
Por cinco espadas.

The Guitar

The cry of the guitar
begins.
The wineglasses of dawn
are broken.
The cry of the guitar
begins.
It's useless
to quiet it.
Impossible
to quiet it.
It cries on monotonously,
the way water cries,
the way wind
cries over a first snowfall.
It's useless
to quiet it.
It cries
for the distance.
For the sand of the incendiary South
that begs for white camellias.
It cries for an arrow without a target,
an afternoon without a morning,
for the first bird
dead on the branch.
Oh guitar!
Heart sorely wounded
by five swords.

EL GRITO

La elipse de un grito
va de monte
a monte.

Desde los olivos,
será un arco iris negro
sobre la noche azul.

¡Ay!

Como un arco de viola,
el grito ha hecho vibrar
largas cuerdas del viento.

¡Ay!

(Las gentes de las cuevas
asoman sus velones.)

¡Ay!

THE CRY

The ellipse of a cry
echoes from mountain
to mountain.

From the olive trees
a black rainbow
veils the blue night.

      Ay!

Like the bow of a viola
the cry vibrates long strings
of wind.

      Ay!

(The cave dwellers'
oil lamps begin to appear.)

      Ay!

El silencio

Oye, hijo mío, el silencio.
Es un silencio ondulado,
un silencio,
donde resbalan valles y ecos
y que inclinan las frentes
hacia el suelo.

THE SILENCE

Can you hear the silence,
my son?
A rolling silence,
a silence,
that leads valleys and echoes astray,
and draws our foreheads
to the ground.

El paso de la Siguiriya

Entre mariposas negras,
va una muchacha morena
junto a una blanca serpiente
de niebla.

Tierra de luz,
cielo de tierra.

Va encadenada al temblor
de un ritmo que nunca llega;
tiene el corazón de plata
y un puñal en la diestra.

¿Adónde vas, Siguiriya,
con un ritmo sin cabeza?
¿Qué luna recogerá
tu dolor de cal y adelfa?

Tierra de luz,
cielo de tierra.

SIGUIRIYA'S WAY

Among black butterflies
a dark-haired girl
walks alongside a white serpent
of fog.

Land of light,
sky of the earth.

She's tied to the tremor
of a rhythm that never arrives;
she has a heart of silver
and in her right hand a dagger.

Where are you going, Siguiriya,
in such mindless rhythm?
Which moon will take in
the whitewash and oleander of your pain?

Land of light,
sky of the earth.

Después de pasar

Los niños miran
un punto lejano.

Los candiles se apagan.
Unas muchachas ciegas
preguntan a la luna,
y por el aire ascienden
espirales de llanto.

Las montañas miran
un punto lejano.

AFTER PASSING

Children
look into the distance.

The oil lamps are extinguished.
Blind young women
question the moon,
and spirals of crying
rise into the air.

Mountains
look into the distance.

Y DESPUÉS

Los laberintos
que crea el tiempo,
se desvanecen.

(Sólo queda
el desierto.)

El corazón,
fuente del deseo,
se desvanece.

(Sólo queda
el desierto.)

La ilusión de la aurora
y los besos,
se desvanecen.

Sólo queda
el desierto.
Un ondulado
desierto.

AND THEN

The labyrinths
that time creates
disappear.

(Only the desert
remains.)

The heart,
that fountain of desire,
disappears.

(Only the desert
remains.)

The illusion of dawn
and of kisses
disappears.

Only the desert
remains.
A rippling
desert.

Poema de la Soleá

A Jorge Zalamea

Tierra seca,
tierra quieta
de noches
inmensas.

(Viento en el olivar,
viento en la sierra.)

Tierra
vieja
del candil
y la pena.
Tierra
de las hondas cisternas.
Tierra
de la muerte sin ojos
y las flechas.

(Viento por los caminos.
Brisa en las alamedas.)

Poem of the Soleá

For Jorge Zalamea

Dry land,
quiet land
of night's
immensity.

(Wind in the olive grove,
wind in the Sierra.)

Ancient
land
of oil lamps
and grief.
Land
of deep cisterns.
Land
of death without eyes
and arrows.

(Wind on the roads.
Breeze in the poplar groves.)

PUEBLO

Sobre el monte pelado,
un calvario.
Agua clara
y olivos centenarios.
Por las callejas
hombres embozados,
y en las torres
veletas girando.
Eternamente
girando.
¡Oh, pueblo perdido,
en la Andalucía del llanto!

VILLAGE

Upon a barren hill,
a Calvary.
Clear water
and century-old olive trees.
In the narrow streets,
men hidden under cloaks,
and on the towers
the spinning vanes.
Forever
spinning.
Oh, village lost
in the Andalucía of tears!

Puñal

El puñal
entra en el corazón,
como la reja del arado
en el yermo.

No.
No me lo claves.
No.

El puñal,
como un rayo de sol,
incendia las terribles
hondonadas.

No.
No me lo claves.
No.

DAGGER

The dagger
enters the heart
the way plowshares turn over
the wasteland.

No.
Do not cut into me.
No.

Like a ray of sun,
the dagger
ignites terrible
hollows.

No.
Do not cut into me.
No.

ENCRUCIJADA

Viento del Este;
un farol
y el puñal
en el corazón.
La calle
tiene un temblor
de cuerda
en tensión,
un temblor
de enorme moscardón.
Por todas partes
yo
veo el puñal
en el corazón.

CROSSROADS

East wind,
a street lamp
and a dagger
in the heart.
The street
quivers like
tightly pulled
string,
like a huge, buzzing
horsefly.
Everywhere,
I see a dagger
in the heart.

¡Ay!

El grito deja en el viento
una sombra de ciprés.

(Dejadme en este campo,
llorando.)

Todo se ha roto en el mundo.
No queda más que el silencio.

(Dejadme en este campo,
llorando.)

El horizonte sin luz
está mordido de hogueras.

(Ya os he dicho que me dejéis
en este campo
llorando.)

Ay!

The cry leaves shadows of cypress
upon the wind.

(Leave me here, in this field,
weeping.)

The whole world's broken.
Only silence remains.

(Leave me here, in this field,
weeping.)

The darkened horizon's
bitten by bonfires.

(I've told you already to leave me
here, in this field,
weeping.)

SORPRESA

Muerto se quedó en la calle
con un puñal en el pecho.
No lo conocía nadie.
¡Cómo temblaba el farol!
Madre.
¡Cómo temblaba el farolito
de la calle!
Era madrugada. Nadie
pudo asomarse a sus ojos
abiertos al duro aire.
Que muerto se quedó en la calle
que con un puñal en el pecho
y que no lo conocía nadie.

SURPRISE

He lay dead in the street
with a dagger in his chest.
Nobody knew who he was.
How the street lamp flickered!
Mother of God,
how the street lamp
faintly flickered!
It was dawn. Nobody
could look up, wide-eyed,
into the glare.
And he lay dead in the street
with a dagger in his chest,
and nobody knew who he was.

La soleá

Vestida con mantos negros
piensa que el mundo es chiquito
y el corazón es inmenso.

Vestida con mantos negros.

Piensa que el suspiro tierno
y el grito, desaparecen
en la corriente del viento.

Vestida con mantos negros.

Se dejó el balcón abierto
y al alba por el balcón
desembocó todo el cielo.

¡Ay yayayayay,
que vestida con mantos negros!

SOLEÁ

Wearing black mantillas,
she thinks the world is tiny
and the heart immense.

Wearing black mantillas.

She thinks that tender sighs
and cries disappear
into currents of wind.

Wearing black mantillas.

The door was left open,
and at dawn the entire sky
emptied onto her balcony.

Ay yayayayay,
wearing black mantillas!

Cueva

De la cueva salen
largos sollozos.

(Lo cárdeno
sobre lo rojo.)

El gitano evoca
países remotos.

(Torres altas y hombres
misteriosos.)

En la voz entrecortada
van sus ojos.

(Lo negro
sobre lo rojo.)

Y la cueva encalada
tiembla en el oro.

(Lo blanco
sobre lo rojo.)

CAVE

From the cave
come endless sobbings.

(Purple
over red.)

The gypsy
calls forth the distance.

(Tall towers
and mysterious men.)

In an unsteady voice
his eyes wander.

(Black
over red.)

And the white-washed cave
trembles in gold.

(White
over red.)

ENCUENTRO

Ni tú ni yo estamos
en disposición
de encontrarnos.
Tú...por lo que ya sabes.
¡Yo la he querido tanto!
Sigue esa veredita.
En las manos
tengo los agujeros
de los clavos.
¿No ves cómo me estoy
desangrando?
No mires nunca atrás,
vete despacio
y reza como yo
a San Cayetano,
que ni tú ni yo estamos
en disposición
de encontrarnos.

ENCOUNTER

For you and I
aren't ready
to find each other.
You ... as you well know.
I loved her so much!
Follow the narrowest path.
I have
holes
in my hands
from the nails.
Can't you see how
I'm bleeding to death?
Don't look back,
go slowly,
and pray as I do
to San Cayetano,
for you and I
aren't ready
to find each other.

ALBA

Campanas de Córdoba
en la madrugada.
Campanas de amanecer
en Granada.
Os sienten todas las muchachas
que lloran a la tierna
Soleá enlutada.
Las muchachas
de Andalucía la alta
y la baja.
Las niñas de España,
de pie menudo
y temblorosas faldas,
que han llenado de luces
las encrucijadas.
¡Oh campanas de Córdoba
en la madrugada,
y oh campanas de amanecer
en Granada!

Dawn

Bells of Córdoba
in the early morning.
Bells of Granada
at dawn.
You are felt by all the girls
who weep to the tender,
weeping Soleá.
The girls
of upper Andalucía,
and of lower.
Young girls of Spain,
with tiny feet
and trembling skirts,
who've filled the crossroads
with lights.
Oh, bells of Córdoba
in the early morning,
and, oh, bells of Granada
at dawn!

Poema de la Saeta

A Francisco Iglesia

ARQUEROS

Los arqueros oscuros
a Sevilla se acercan.

Guadalquivir abierto.

Anchos sombreros grises,
largas capas lentas.

¡Ay, Guadalquivir!

Vienen de los remotos
países de la pena.

Guadalquivir abierto.

Y van a un laberinto.
Amor, cristal y piedra.

¡Ay, Guadalquivir!

Poem of the Saeta

For Francisco Iglesias

ARCHERS

Unseen archers
are approaching Sevilla.

Guadalquivir, open to the sea.

Broad, gray hats.
Long, trailing cloaks.

Ay, Guadalquivir!

They come from remote
countries of grief.

Guadalquivir, open to the sea.

And they're entering a labyrinth.
Love, crystal, and stone.

¡Ay, Guadalquivir!

NOCHE

Cirio, candil,
farol y luciérnaga.

La constelación
de la Saeta.

Ventanitas de oro
tiemblan,
y en la aurora se mecen
cruces superpuestas.

Cirio, candil,
farol y luciérnaga.

NIGHT

Candle, oil lamp,
street lamp, firefly.

The constellation
of the Saeta.

Small gold windows
shudder,
and crosses
sway upon the dawn.

Candle, oil lamp,
street lamp, firefly.

SEVILLA

Sevilla es una torre
llena de arqueros finos.

Sevilla para herir.
Córdoba para morir.

Una ciudad que acecha
largos ritmos,
y los enrosca
como laberintos.
Como tallos de parra
encendidos.

¡Sevilla para herir!

Bajo el arco del cielo,
sobre su llano limpio,
dispara la constante
saeta de su río.

¡Córdoba para morir!

Y loca de horizonte
mezcla en su vino,
lo amargo de Don Juan
y lo perfecto de Dionisio.

Sevilla para herir.
¡Siempre Sevilla para herir!

SEVILLA

Sevilla is a tower
full of highly skilled archers.

Sevilla for wounding.
Córdoba for dying.

A city that ambushes
lengthy rhythms,
and coils them up
like labyrinths.
Like flaming
grapevines.

Sevilla for wounding!

Beneath the arc of the sky,
above its clean plain,
it lets fly the constant
Saeta of its river.

Córdoba for dying!

And crazed by the horizon
it mixes in its own wine
the bitterness of Don Juan
and Dionysian perfection.

Sevilla for wounding.
Sevilla, forever, for wounding!

PROCESIÓN

Por la calleja vienen
extraños unicornios.
¿De qué campo,
de qué bosque mitológico?
Más cerca,
ya parecen astrónomos.
Fantásticos Merlines
y el Ecce Homo,
Durandarte encantado,
Orlando furioso.

PROCESSION

Strange unicorns
parade the narrow streets.
From what field,
from what mythological forest?
Closer still,
they appear to be astronomers.
Fantastic Merlins
and the Ecce Homo,
an enchanted Durandarte,
a furious Orlando.

Paso

Virgen con miriñaque,
virgen de la Soledad,
abierta como un inmenso
tulipán.
En tu barco de luces
vas
por la alta marea
de la ciudad,
entre saetas turbias
y estrellas de cristal.
Virgen con miriñaque
tú vas
por el río de la calle,
¡hasta el mar!

THE WAY

Virgin in crinoline,
opened up like an enormous
tulip,
Virgin of Solitude.
In your boat of light,
among turbulent Saetas
and crystal stars,
you sail
the high tide of the city.
Virgin in crinoline,
you sail
upon the river of the street
until you reach the sea!

SAETA

Cristo moreno
pasa
de lirio de Judea
a clavel de España.

¡Miradlo, por dónde viene!

De España.
Cielo limpio y oscuro,
tierra tostada,
y cauces donde corre
muy lenta el agua.
Cristo moreno,
con las guedejas quemadas,
los pómulos salientes
y las pupilas blancas.

¡Miradlo, por dónde va!

SAETA

A black Christ
changes from a lily of Judea
to a carnation of Spain.

Look where he comes from!

From Spain.
A clear, dark sky,
a scorched earth,
and riverbeds in which
the waters move slowly.
A black Christ
with long, blackened hair,
prominent cheekbones,
white eyes.

Look where he's going!

BALCÓN

La Lola
canta saetas.
Los toreritos
la rodean,
y el barberillo
desde su puerta,
sigue los ritmos
con la cabeza.
Entre la albahaca
y la hierbabuena,
la Lola canta
saetas.
La Lola aquella,
que se miraba
tanto en la alberca.

BALCONY

Lola
is singing Saetas.
Young bullfighters
circle her,
and the young barber,
in his doorway,
nods to the rhythm
with his head.
Among sweet basil
and mint,
Lola is singing
Saetas.
That Lola,
who had so admired
herself in the pool.

Madrugada

Pero como el amor
los saeteros
están ciegos.

Sobre la noche verde,
las saetas
dejan rastros de lirio
caliente.

La quilla de la luna
rompe nubes moradas
y las aljabas
se llenan de rocío.

¡Ay, pero como el amor
los saeteros
están ciegos!

Early Morning

But like love,
the archers
are blind.

Upon the green night,
their Saetas
leave traces of warm
lily.

The keel of the moon
breaks through purple clouds,
and their quivers
fill with dew.

Ay, but like love,
the archers
are blind.

Gráfico de la Petenera

A Eugenio Montes

CAMPANA

(Bordón)

En la torre
amarilla,
dobla una campana.

Sobre el viento
amarillo
se abren las campanadas.

En la torre
amarilla
cesa la campana.

El viento con el polvo
hace proras de plata.

Description of the Petenera

For Eugenio Montes

BELL
(Bass String)

In the yellow
tower,
a bell tolls.

Upon the yellow
wind
the pealing breaks out.

In the yellow
tower,
the bell stops tolling.

The wind and the dust
fashion prows of silver.

CAMINO

Cien jinetes enlutados,
¿dónde irán,
por el cielo yacente
del naranjal?
Ni a Córdoba ni a Sevilla
llegarán.
Ni a Granada la que suspira
por el mar.
Esos caballos soñolientos
los llevarán
al laberinto de las cruces
donde tiembla el cantar.
Con siete ayes clavados,
¿dónde irán,
los cien jinetes andaluces
del naranjal?

ROAD

A hundred horsemen in funeral attire,
where will they go
in the laid-to-rest heavens
of the orange grove?
Neither Córdoba nor Sevilla
is reachable.
Nor Granada, which sighs
for the sea.
Those drowsy horses
will take them
to a labyrinth of crosses
where the song shudders so.
Pierced by seven ays,
where will they go,
the hundred Andalucían horsemen
of the orange grove?

LAS SEIS CUERDAS

La guitarra
hace llorar a los sueños.
El sollozo de las almas
perdidas
se escapa por su boca
redonda.
Y como la tarántula,
teje una gran estrella
para cazar suspiros,
que flotan en su negro
aljibe de madera.

Six Strings

The guitar
makes dreams cry.
The sobbing of lost
souls
escapes through its round
mouth.
And like the tarantula,
it spins a huge star
and tracks down the sighs
that float in its black
wooden cistern.

Danza

(En el huerto de la Petenera)

En la noche del huerto,
seis gitanas
vestidas de blanco
bailan.

En la noche del huerto,
coronadas
con rosas de papel
y biznagas.

En la noche del huerto,
sus dientes de nácar
escriben la sombra
quemada.

Y en la noche del huerto,
sus sombras se alargan,
y llegan hasta el cielo
moradas.

DANCE

(In the Garden of the Petenera)

At night, in the garden,
six gypsies
in white dresses
are dancing.

At night, in the garden,
crowned
with paper roses
and sprigs of jasmine.

At night, in the garden,
their pearl-colored teeth
inscribe the scorched
shadow.

And at night, in the garden,
their shadows lengthen
until, purple-colored,
they reach the sky.

Muerte de la Petenera

En la casa blanca muere
la perdición de los hombres.

Cien jacas caracolean.
Sus jinetes están muertos.

Bajo las estremecidas
estrellas de los velones,
su falda de moaré tiembla
entre sus muslos de cobre.

Cien jacas caracolean.
Sus jinetes están muertos.

Largas sombras afiladas
vienen del turbio horizonte,
y el bordón de una guitarra
se rompe.

Cien jacas caracolean.
Sus jinetes están muertos.

DEATH OF THE PETENERA

In this white house
human perdition dies.

A hundred ponies are prancing.
Their riders are all dead.

Beneath the flickering
stars of the oil lamps,
her silken skirt trembles
between her copper thighs.

A hundred ponies are prancing.
Their riders are all dead.

Long, sharpened shadows
descend from a cloud-filled horizon,
and a guitar's bass string
snaps.

A hundred ponies are prancing.
Their riders are all dead.

Falseta

¡Ay, Petenera gitana!
¡Yayay Petenera!
Tu entierro no tuvo niñas
buenas.
Niñas que le dan a Cristo muerto
sus guedejas,
y llevan blancas mantillas
en las ferias.
Tu entierro fue de gente
siniestra.
Gente con el corazón
en la cabeza,
que te siguió llorando
por las callejas.
¡Ay, Petenera gitana!
¡Yayay Petenera!

FLOURISH

Ay, gypsy Petenera!
Yayay Petenera!
Good little girls did not attend
your burial.
Girls who offer their locks
to the dead Christ,
and who wear white scarves
in the open markets.
Your burial was attended
by sinister people.
People whose hearts
exist only in their minds,
and who followed you, weeping,
through the narrow streets.
Ay, gypsy Petenera!
Yayay Petenera!

DE PROFUNDIS

Los cien enamorados
duerman para siempre
bajo la tierra seca.
Andalucía tiene
largos caminos rojos.
Córdoba, olivos verdes
donde poner cien cruces,
que los recuerden.
Los cien enamorados
duermen para siempre.

DE PROFUNDIS

A hundred lovers
sleep forever
beneath this dry land.
Andalusia,
long, red-colored roads.
Córdoba, green olive trees,
where a hundred crosses
are placed in their memory.
A hundred lovers
sleep forever.

CLAMOR

En las torres
amarillas
doblan las campanas.

Sobre los vientos
amarillos
se abren las campanadas.

Por un camino va
la Muerte, coronada
de azahares marchitos.
Canta y canta
una canción
en su vihuela blanca,
y canta y canta y canta.

En las torres amarillas,
cesan las campanas.

El viento con el polvo,
hace proras de plata.

CLAMOR

In the yellow
towers,
the bells toll.

Upon the yellow
winds,
the pealing breaks out.

Death, crowned with
withered orange blossoms,
travels down a road.
She sings and sings
a song
with her ancient white guitar,
and sings and sings and sings.

In the yellow towers,
the bells stop tolling.

The wind and the dust
fashion prows of silver.

Dos muchachas

A Máximo Quijano

La Lola

Bajo el naranjo lava
pañales de algodón.
Tiene verdes los ojos
y violeta la voz.

¡Ay, amor,
bajo el naranjo en flor!

El agua de la acequia
iba llena de sol.
En el olivarito
cantaba un gorrión.

¡Ay, amor,
bajo el naranjo en flor!

Luego, cuando la Lola
gaste todo el jabón,
vendrán los torerillos.

¡Ay, amor,
bajo el naranjo en flor!

Two Young Women

For Máximo Quijano

LOLA

Under the orange tree
she washes cotton diapers.
She has green eyes
and a violet voice.

Ay, love,
under the blossoming orange!

The water flowing in the ditch
was filled with sunlight.
A sparrow was singing
in a little olive grove.

Ay, love,
under the blossoming orange!

And later, when Lola
runs out of soap,
young bullfighters arrive.

Ay, love,
under the blossoming orange!

Amparo

Amparo,
¡qué sola estás en tu casa
vestida de blanco!

(Ecuador entre el jazmín
y el nardo.)

Oyes los maravillosos
surtidores de tu patio,
y el débil trino amarillo
del canario.

Por la tarde ves temblar
los cipreses con los pájaros,
mientras bordas lentamente
letras sobre el cañamazo.

Amparo,
¡qué sola estás en tu casa
vestida de blanco!

Amparo,
¡y qué difícil decirte:
yo te amo!

AMPARO

How alone you are in your own home,
Amparo,
all dressed in white!

(Like the difference between jasmine
and spikenard.)

You listen to the marvelous
fountains of your courtyard,
and the fragile, yellow trilling
of the canary.

In the evening, you watch
cypresses tremble with birds,
while you ever-so-slowly
embroider letters upon the canvas.

How alone you are in your own home,
Amparo,
all dressed in white!

And how difficult to tell you,
Amparo,
that I love you!

Viñetas flamencas

A Manuel Torre, "Niño de Jerez," que tiene tronco de Faraón

RETRATO DE SILVERIO FRANCONETTI

Entre italiano
y flamenco,
¿cómo cantaría
aquel Silverio?
La densa miel de Italia,
con el limón nuestro,
iba en el hondo llanto
del siguiriyero.
Su grito fue terrible.
Los viejos
dicen que se erizaban
los cabellos,
y se abría el azogue
de los espejos.
Pasaba por los tonos
sin romperlos.

Y fue un creador
y un jardinero.
Un creador de glorietas
para el silencio.

Ahora su melodía
duerme con los ecos.
Definitiva y pura.
¡Con los últimos ecos!

76

Flamenco Vignettes

For Manuel Torre, "Niño de Jerez," who has the body of a Pharoah

PORTRAIT OF SILVERIO FRANCONETTI

Between Italian
and flamenco,
how would that Silverio
have sung?
The thick honey of Italy,
mixed with our lemon,
flowed through the deep wail
of his Siguiriya.
His cry was terrifying.
The old folk
say that one's hair
stood on end,
and that quicksilver
splintered the mirrors.
He shifted tonality
with ease.

He was an artist.
And he was a gardener.
A creator of arbors
for silence.

Now his melody
sleeps with echoes.
Definitive and pure.
With the ultimate echoes!

JUAN BREVA

Juan Breva tenía
cuerpo de gigante
y voz de niña.
Nada como su trino.
Era la misma
Pena cantando
detrás de una sonrisa.
Evoca los limonares
de Málaga la dormida,
y hay en su llanto dejos
de sal marina.
Como Homero cantó
ciego. Su voz tenía
algo de mar sin luz
y naranja exprimida.

JUAN BREVA

Juan Breva was possessed
with the body of a giant
and the voice of a little girl.
His trill was unique.
It was the same grief
that was sung
behind his smile.
It recalled the lemon groves
of sleepy Málaga,
and in his cry
was a slight taste of sea salt.
Like Homer, he sang blind.
His voice was possessed,
a trace of the sea without light
and the squeezed orange.

CAFÉ CANTANTE

Lámparas de cristal
y espejos verdes.

Sobre el tablado oscuro,
la Parrala sostiene
una conversación
con la muerte.
La llama,
no viene,
y la vuelve a llamar.
Las gentes
aspiran los sollozos.
Y en los espejos verdes,
largas colas de seda
se mueven.

CAFÉ FLAMENCO

Lamps of crystal
and green mirrors.

On a dark stage
Parrala maintains
a conversation
with Death.
She calls out to Death,
but Death never answers her,
and she calls out again.
The audience
inhales her sobbings.
And in those green mirrors
her long, silken dress
is swaying.

LAMENTACIÓN DE LA MUERTE

A Miguel Benítez

Sobre el cielo negro,
culebrinas amarillas.

Vine a este mundo con ojos
y me voy sin ellos.
¡Señor del mayor dolor!
Y luego,
un velón y una manta
en el suelo.

Quise llegar adonde
llegaron los buenos.
¡Y he llegado, Dios mío!...
Pero luego,
un velón y una manta
en el suelo.

Limoncito amarillo,
limonero.
Echad los limoncitos
al viento.
¡Ya lo sabéis!... Porque luego,
luego,
un velón y una manta
en el suelo.

Sobre el cielo negro,
culebrinas amarillas.

LAMENTATION OF DEATH

For Miguel Benítez

All across the black sky,
yellow, snakelike flashes.

I came into this world with eyes,
and I'll leave without them.
Oh, Lord of Greatest Sorrow!
And then,
an oil lamp and a blanket
upon the ground.

I wanted to go
where the blessed people go.
And I have, dear God...!
But then,
an oil lamp and a blanket
upon the ground.

Tiny, yellow lemon.
Lemon tree.
Cast your tiny lemons
to the wind.
Now you get it...! Because then,
then,
an oil lamp and a blanket
upon the ground.

All across the black sky,
yellow, snakelike flashes.

Conjuro

La mano crispada
como una Medusa
ciega el ojo doliente
del candil.

As de bastos.
Tijeras en cruz.

Sobre el humo blanco
del incienso, tiene
algo de topo y
mariposa indecisa.

As de bastos.
Tijeras en cruz.

Aprieta un corazón
invisible, ¿la veis?
Un corazón
reflejado en el viento.

As de bastos.
Tijeras en cruz.

Exorcism

The twitching hand,
like Medusa,
blinds the aching eye
of the oil lamp.

Ace of clubs.
Open scissors in a cross.

In the white smoke
of the incense, it resembles
a mole
and an uncertain butterfly.

Ace of clubs.
Open scissors in a cross.

An invisible heart
is in trouble. Can you see it?
A heart reflected
on the wind.

Ace of clubs.
Open scissors in a cross.

MEMENTO

Cuando yo me muera,
enterradme con mi guitarra
bajo la arena.

Cuando yo me muera,
entre los naranjos
y la hierbabuena.

Cuando yo me muera,
enterradme, si queréis,
en una veleta.

¡Cuando yo me muera!

MEMENTO

When I die,
bury me with my guitar
beneath the sand.

When I die,
among orange trees
and mint.

When I die,
bury me, if you care to,
in a weather vane.

When I die!

Tres ciudades

A Pilar Zubiaurre

MALAGUEÑA

La muerte
entra y sale
de la taberna.

Pasan caballos negros
y gente siniestra
por los hondos caminos
de la guitarra.

Y hay un olor a sal
y a sangre de hembra
en los nardos febriles
de la marina.

La muerte
entra y sale
y sale y entra,
la muerte
de la taberna.

Three Cities

For Pilar Zubiaurre

MALAGUEÑA

Death
goes in and out
of the tavern.

Black horses
and sinister people
travel the deep roads
of the guitar.

And there's a smell of salt
and menstrual blood
in the feverish spikenard
at the shore.

Death
goes in and out,
and out of, and into
the tavern goes
death.

Barrio de Córdoba

(Tópico nocturno)

En la casa se defienden
de las estrellas.
La noche se derrumba.
Dentro hay una niña muerta
con una rosa encarnada
oculta en la cabellera.
Seis ruiseñores la lloran
en la reja.

Las gentes van suspirando
con las guitarras abiertas.

CÓRDOBA BARRIO

(Nocturnal Theme)

In that house, they defend themselves
against the stars.
The night is thrown down.
Inside, there is a young, dead girl
with a flesh-colored rose
hidden in her hair.
On the bars of her window,
six nightingales mourn for her.

Displaying their guitars,
everyone sighs.

BAILE

La Carmen está bailando
por las calles de Sevilla.
Tiene blancos los cabellos
y brillantes las pupilas.

¡Niñas,
corred las cortinas!

En su cabeza se enrosca
una serpiente amarilla,
y va soñando en el baile
con galanes de otros días.

¡Niñas,
corred las cortinas!

Las calles están desiertas
y en los fondos se adivinan
corazones andaluces
buscando viejas espinas.

¡Niñas,
corred las cortinas!

DANCE

Carmen is dancing
down the streets of Sevilla.
She has long, white curls
and brilliant eyes.

Little girls,
close the curtains!

A yellow snake is coiled
in her mind,
and she dreams that she's dancing
with lovers of days gone by.

Little girls,
close the curtains!

The streets are deserted,
but in the background Andalucían hearts,
in search of ancient thorns,
are uncovered.

Little girls,
close the curtains!

Seis caprichos

A Regino Sainz de la Maza

ADIVINANZA DE LA GUITARRA

En la redonda
encrucijada,
seis doncellas
bailan.
Tres de carne
y tres de plata.
Los sueños de ayer las buscan,
pero las tiene abrazadas
un Polifemo de oro.
¡La guitarra!

Six Caprices

For Regino Sainz de la Maza

RIDDLE OF THE GUITAR

On the roundabout
at the crossroads,
six virgins
are dancing.
Three of flesh
and three of silver.
Yesterday's dreams look for them,
but a golden Polyphemus
embraces them.
Oh, guitar!

CANDIL

¡Oh, qué grave medita
la llama del candil!

Como un faquir indio
mira su entraña de oro
y se eclipsa soñando
atmósferas sin viento.

Cigüeña incandescente
pica desde su nido
a las sombras macizas
y se asoma temblando
a los ojos redondos
del gitanillo muerto.

Oil Lamp

Oh, how gravely the flame
of the oil lamp meditates!

Like an Indian fakir,
it beholds its own golden center,
and then is eclipsed, dreaming
windless atmospheres.

An incandescent stork
pecks at the massive shadows
from inside its nest,
and, trembling, peeks
into the round eyes
of a young, dead gypsy.

CRÓTALO

Crótalo.
Crótalo.
Crótalo.
Escarabajo sonoro.

En la araña
de la mano
rizas el aire
cálido
y te ahogas en tu trino
de palo.

Crótalo.
Crótalo.
Crótalo.
Escarabajo sonoro.

CASTANET

Castanet.
Castanet.
Castanet.
Sonorous beetle.

In the spider
of the hand,
you ripple
the warm air,
and you drown
in your wooden trill.

Castanet.
Castanet.
Castanet.
Sonorous beetle.

CHUMBERA

Laocoonte salvaje.

¡Qué bien estás
bajo la media luna!

Múltiple pelotari.

¡Qué bien estás
amenazando al viento!

Dafne y Atis,
saben de tu dolor.
Inexplicable.

Prickly Pear

Wild Laocoön.

How comfortable you are
beneath the half-moon!

Many-armed handball player.

How comfortable you are,
threatening the wind!

Daphne and Attis
know all about your pain.
Inexplicable.

PITA

Pulpo petrificado.

Pones cinchas cenicientas
al vientre de los montes
y muelas formidables
a los desfiladeros.

Pulpo petrificado.

MAGUEY PLANT

Petrified octopus.

You put ashen cinches
on the bellies of mountains
and formidable molars
in their narrow passes.

Petrified octopus.

CRUZ

La cruz.
(Punto final
del camino.)

Se mira en la acequia.
(Puntos suspensivos.)

CROSS

The cross.
(Last stop
on the road.)

It looks at itself in the ditch.
(Last stops, suspended.)

Escena del teniente coronel
de la Guardia Civil

Cuarto de banderas

TENIENTE CORONEL: Yo soy el teniente coronel de la Guardia Civil.

SARGENTO: Sí.

TENIENTE CORONEL: Y no hay quien me desmienta.

SARGENTO: No.

TENIENTE CORONEL: Tengo tres estrellas y veinte cruces.

SARGENTO: Sí.

TENIENTE CORONEL: Me ha saludado el cardenal arzobispo de
Toledo con sus veinticuatro borlas moradas.

SARGENTO: Sí.

TENIENTE CORONEL: Yo soy el teniente. Yo soy el teniente. Yo soy el
teniente coronel de la Guardia Civil.

*(Romeo y Julieta, celeste, blanco y oro, se abrazan sobre el jardín de tabaco
de la caja de puros. El militar acaricia el cañón de su fusil lleno de sombra
submarina.)*

Scene of the Lieutenant Colonel
of the Civil Guard

GUARD ROOM

LIEUTENANT COLONEL: I am the Lieutenant Colonel of the Civil Guard.

SERGEANT: Yes, sir.

LIEUTENANT COLONEL: And nobody contradicts me.

SERGEANT: No, sir.

LIEUTENANT COLONEL: I have three stars and twenty crosses.

SERGEANT: Yes, sir.

LIEUTENANT COLONEL: The Cardinal Archbishop of Toledo has greeted
me with his twenty-four purple tassles.

SERGEANT: Yes, sir.

LIEUTENANT COLONEL: I am the Lieutenant. I am the Lieutenant. I am
the Lieutenant Colonel of the Civil Guard.

*(Romeo and Juliet, celestially, white and gold, embrace above the tobacco
garden of a cigar box. The soldier caresses the barrel of his gun, filled with
submarine darkness.)*

UNA VOZ *(fuera):* Luna, luna, luna, luna,
del tiempo de la aceituna.
Cazorla enseña su torre
y Benamejí la oculta.

Luna, luna, luna, luna.
Un gallo canta en la luna.
Señor alcalde, sus niñas
están mirando a la luna.

TENIENTE CORONEL: ¿Qué pasa?

SARGENTO: ¡Un gitano!

(La mirada de mulo joven del gitanillo *ensombrece y agiganta los* ojirris *del* teniente coronel *de la Guardia Civil.)*

TENIENTE CORONEL: Yo soy el teniente de la Guardia Civil.

SARGENTO: Sí.

TENIENTE CORONEL: ¿Tú, quién eres?

GITANO: Un gitano.

TENIENTE CORONEL: ¿Y qué es un gitano?

GITANO: Cualquier cosa.

TENIENTE CORONEL: ¿Cómo te llamas?

GITANO: Eso.

A Voice *(off-stage):* Moon, moon, moon, moon,
of the olive's harvest moon.
Cazorla reveals her tower,
and Benamejí conceals it.

Moon, moon, moon, moon,
a rooster crows in the moon.
Mr. Mayor, your daughters
are looking up at the moon.

Lieutenant Colonel: What's happening?

Sergeant: A gypsy, sir!

(The mulish gaze of a young Gypsy *causes the beady little eyes of the* Lieutenant Colonel *of the Civil Guard to widen and darken.)*

Lieutenant Colonel: I am the Lieutenant Colonel of the Civil Guard.

Gypsy: Yes.

Lieutenant Colonel: And you, who are you?

Gypsy: A gypsy.

Lieutenant Colonel: And what is a gypsy?

Gypsy: Whatever.

Lieutenant Colonel: So what is your name?

Gypsy: Just that.

TENIENTE CORONEL: ¿Qué dices?

GITANO: Gitano.

SARGENTO: Me lo encontré y lo he traído.

TENIENTE CORONEL: ¿Dónde estabas?

GITANO: En la puente de los ríos.

TENIENTE CORONEL: Pero ¿de qué ríos?

GITANO: De todos los ríos.

TENIENTE CORONEL: ¿Y qué hacías allí?

GITANO: Una torre de canela.

TENIENTE CORONEL: ¡Sargento!

SARGENTO: A la orden, mi teniente coronel de la Guardia Civil.

GITANO: He inventado unas alas para volar, y vuelo. Azufre y
rosas en mis labios.

TENIENTE CORONEL: ¡Ay!

GITANO: Aunque no necesito alas, porque vuelo sin ellas.
Nubes y anillos en mi sangre.

TENIENTE CORONEL: ¡Ayyy!

LIEUTENANT COLONEL: What did you say?

GYPSY: Gypsy.

SERGEANT: I found him, and so I brought him here, sir.

LIEUTENANT COLONEL: Where were you?

GYPSY: On a bridge over the rivers.

LIEUTENANT COLONEL: But over which rivers?

GYPSY: Over all the rivers.

LIEUTENANT COLONEL: And what were you doing there?

GYPSY: Building a tower of cinnamon.

LIEUTENANT COLONEL: Sergeant!

SERGEANT: At your command, Lieutenant Colonel of the Civil
            Guard, sir.

GYPSY: I constructed wings for flying, and so I fly. Sulfur and rose
        upon my lips.

LIEUTENANT COLONEL: Ay!

GYPSY: Though I don't really need wings, because I can fly
        without them. Clouds and rings are in my blood.

LIEUTENANT COLONEL: Ayyy!

GITANO: En enero tengo azahar.

TENIENTE CORONEL *(retorciéndose):* ¡Ayyyyy!

GITANO: Y naranjas en la nieve.

TENIENTE CORONEL: ¡Ayyyyy, pun, pin, pam! *(Cae muerto.)*

(El alma de tabaco y café con leche del teniente coronel de la Guardia Civil sale por la ventana.)

SARGENTO: ¡Socorro!

(En el patio del cuartel, cuatro guardias civiles apalean al gitanillo.)

GYPSY: In January, I have orange blossoms.

LIEUTENANT COLONEL (*backing away*): Ayyyyy!

GYPSY: And oranges in the falling snow.

LIEUTENANT COLONEL: Ayyyyy! Boom, bam, bang. (*He falls down dead.*)

(*The Lieutenant Colonel of the Civil Guard's tobacco and café con leche soul flies out the window.*)

SERGEANT: Help!

(*In the barracks yard, four civil guardsmen are beating the young Gypsy.*)

Canción del gitano apaleado

Veinticuatro bofetadas.
Veinticinco bofetadas;
después, mi madre, a la noche,
me pondrá en papel de plata.

Guardia Civil caminera,
dadme unos sorbitos de agua.
Agua con peces y barcos.
Agua, agua, agua, agua.

¡Ay, mandor de los civiles
que estás arriba en tu sala!
¡No habrá pañuelos de seda
para limpiarme la cara!

5 de julio 1925

Song of the Beaten Gypsy

Twenty-four blows...
Twenty-five blows...
Later tonight, my mother
will lay me down on silver paper.

Civil guardsmen of the roads,
give me a few swallows of water.
Water with fish and with boats.
Water, water, water, water.

Ay, Civil Guard Commander.
You, up there in your living room!
I'll never have silken handkerchiefs
with which to clean my face!

July 5, 1925

Diálogo del Amargo

Una voz: Amargo.
      Las adelfas de mi patio.
      Corazón de almendra amarga.
      Amargo.

(Llegan tres jóvenes con anchos sombreros.)

Joven 1: Vamos a llegar tarde.

Joven 2: La noche se nos echa encima.

Joven 1: ¿Y ése?

Joven 2: Viene detrás.

Joven 1 *(en alta voz)*: ¡Amargo!

Amargo *(lejos)*: Ya voy.

Joven 2 *(a voces)*: ¡Amargo!

Amargo *(con calma)*: ¡Ya voy!

(Pausa)

Dialogue of Amargo the Bitter

COUNTRYSIDE

A VOICE: Amargo.
      The oleander of my courtyard.
      Heart of bitter almond.
      Amargo.

(Three young men with wide-brimmed hats arrive.)

1ST YOUNG MAN: We're going to get there late.

2ND YOUNG MAN: The night falls all around us.

1ST YOUNG MAN: And him?

2ND YOUNG MAN: He's coming along behind us.

1ST YOUNG MAN *(in a loud voice)*: Amargo!

AMARGO *(far off)*: I'm coming.

2ND YOUNG MAN *(loudly)*: Amargo!

AMARGO *(calmly)*: I'm coming!

(Pause)

Joven 1: ¡Qué hermosos olivares!

Joven 2: Sí.

(*Largo silencio*)

Joven 1: No me gusta andar de noche.

Joven 2: Ni a mí tampoco.

Joven 1: La noche se hizo para dormir.

Joven 2: Es verdad.

(*Ranas y grillos hacen la glorieta del estío andaluz. El Amargo camina con las manos en la cintura.*)

Amargo: Ay yayayay.
        Yo le pregunté a la muerte.
        Ay yayayay.

(*El grito de su canto pone un acento circunflejo sobre el corazón de los que le han oído.*)

Joven 1 (*desde muy lejos*): ¡Amargo!

Joven 2 (*casi perdido*): ¡Amargooo!

(*Silencio*)

(*El Amargo está solo en medio de la carretera. Entorna sus grandes ojos verdes y se ciñe la chaqueta de pana alrededor del talle. Altas*

1ST YOUNG MAN: What beautiful olive groves!

2ND YOUNG MAN: Yes.

(A long silence)

1ST YOUNG MAN: I don't like traveling at night.

2ND YOUNG MAN: Neither do I.

1ST YOUNG MAN: The night was made for sleeping.

2ND YOUNG MAN: It's true.

(Frogs and crickets make up the arbor of Andalucían summer. Amargo walks with his hands on his hips.)

AMARGO: Ay yayayay.
       I asked Death a question.
       Ay yayayay.

(The hearts of the two young men who have heard him are turned toward him by the cry of his song.)

1ST YOUNG MAN: *(from very far off)*: Amargo!

2ND YOUNG MAN *(almost lost)*: Amargo-o-o!

(Silence)

(Amargo *is alone in the middle of the road. He half-closes his large green eyes, and pulls his corduroy jacket tight around his waist. Tall*

montañas le rodean. Su gran reloj de plata le suena oscuramente en el bolsillo a cada paso.)

(Un jinete *viene galopando por la carretera.)*

JINETE *(parando el caballo):* ¡Buenas noches!

AMARGO: A la paz de Dios.

JINETE: ¿Va usted a Granada?

AMARGO: A Granada voy.

JINETE: Pues vamos juntos.

AMARGO: Eso parece.

JINETE: ¿Por qué no monta en la grupa?

AMARGO: Porque no me duelen los pies.

JINETE: Yo vengo de Málaga.

AMARGO: Bueno.

JINETE: Allí están mis hermanos.

AMARGO *(displicente):* ¿Cuántos?

JINETE: Son tres. Venden cuchillos. Ése es el negocio.

AMARGO: De salud les sirva.

mountains surround him. His large silver watch ticks darkly with each step.)

(A Horseman *comes galloping down the road.)*

HORSEMAN *(stopping his horse):* Good evening!

AMARGO: Peace be to God.

HORSEMAN: Are you going to Granada?

AMARGO: I'm going to Granada.

HORSEMAN: Well, let's go together.

AMARGO: I suppose so.

HORSEMAN: Why don't you climb up on back?

AMARGO: Because my feet aren't tired.

HORSEMAN: I'm coming from Málaga.

AMARGO: That's nice.

HORSEMAN: My brothers are there.

AMARGO *(disagreeably):* How many?

HORSEMAN: There are three of them. They sell knives. That's their trade.

AMARGO: May it bring them good health.

JINETE: De plata y de oro.

AMARGO: Un cuchillo no tiene que ser más que cuchillo.

JINETE: Se equivoca.

AMARGO: Gracias.

JINETE: Los cuchillos de oro se van solos al corazón. Los de plata cortan el cuello como una brizna de hierba.

AMARGO: ¿No sirven para partir el pan?

JINETE: Los hombres parten el pan con las manos.

AMARGO: ¡Es verdad!

(*El caballo se inquieta.*)

JINETE: ¡Caballo!

AMARGO: Es la noche.

(*El camino ondulante salomoniza la sombra del animal.*)

JINETE: ¿Quieres un cuchillo?

AMARGO: No.

JINETE: Mira que te lo regalo.

AMARGO: Pero yo no lo acepto.

HORSEMAN: Knives of silver and gold.

AMARGO: A knife is a knife, and nothing more.

HORSEMAN: Ah, but you are mistaken.

AMARGO: Thanks for telling me.

HORSEMAN: Gold knives slip into the heart by themselves. And silver ones cut a throat as if it were a blade of grass.

AMARGO: Can they not even slice bread?

HORSEMAN: Men break bread with their hands.

AMARGO: It's true!

(*The horse grows restless.*)

HORSEMAN: Horse!

AMARGO: It's just the night.

(*The uneven road distorts the animal's shadow.*)

HORSEMAN: Would you like to have a knife?

AMARGO: No.

HORSEMAN: Here, I'll give one to you.

AMARGO: But I won't accept it.

JINETE: No tendrás otra ocasión.

AMARGO: ¿Quién sabe?

JINETE: Los otros cuchillos no sirven. Los otros cuchillos son blandos y se asustan de la sangre. Los que nosotros vendemos son fríos. ¿Entiendes? Entran buscando el sitio de más calor y allí se paran.

(El Amargo calla. Su mano derecha se le enfría como si agarrase un pedazo de oro.)

JINETE : ¡Qué hermoso cuchillo!

AMARGO: ¿Vale mucho?

JINETE: Pero ¿no quieres éste?

(Saca un cuchillo de oro. La punta brilla como una llama de candil.)

AMARGO: He dicho que no.

JINETE: ¡Muchacho, súbete conmigo!

AMARGO: Todavía no estoy cansado.

(El caballo se vuelve a espantar.)

JINETE *(tirando de las bridas)*: Pero ¡qué caballo éste!

AMARGO: Es lo oscuro.

HORSEMAN: But you won't have another opportunity.

AMARGO: Who knows?

HORSEMAN: Other knives aren't any good. They're soft, and afraid of blood. The knives we sell are ice cold. Understand? They enter looking for the warmest spot, and there they stop.

(Amargo *grows quiet. His right hand turns cold, as if he were clutching a piece of gold.*)

HORSEMAN: What a beautiful knife!

AMARGO: Is it worth a great deal?

HORSEMAN: But wouldn't you rather like this one?

(*He pulls out a gold knife. Its tip shines like the flame of an oil lamp.*)

AMARGO: I told you, no.

HORSEMAN: Climb up here with me, my friend.

AMARGO: I'm still not tired.

(*The horse starts to bolt again.*)

HORSEMAN (*pulling on the reins*): But what a horse this is!

AMARGO: It's only the dark.

(Pausa)

JINETE: Como te iba diciendo, en Málaga están mis tres
  hermanos. ¡Qué manera de vender cuchillos! En la
  catedral compraron dos mil para adornar todos los altares
  y poner una corona a la torre. Muchos barcos escribieron
  en ellos sus nombres; los pescadores más humildes de la
  orilla del mar se alumbran de noche con el brillo que
  despiden sus hojas afiladas.

AMARGO: ¡Es una hermosura!

JINETE: ¿Quién lo puede negar?

*(La noche se espesa como un vino de cien años. La serpiente gorda del
Sur abre sus ojos en la madrugada, y hay en los durmientes un deseo
infinito de arrojarse por el balcón a la magia perversa del perfume y la
lejanía.)*

AMARGO: Me parece que hemos perdido el camino.

JINETE *(parando el caballo)*: ¿Sí?

AMARGO: Con la conversación.

JINETE: ¿No son aquéllas las luces de Granada?

AMARGO: No sé. El mundo es muy grande.

JINETE: Y muy solo.

AMARGO: Como que está deshabitado.

(*Pause*)

HORSEMAN: As I was telling you, my three brothers are in Málaga. What a way of selling knives they have! At the cathedral, they bought two thousand, just so they might adorn all the altars and place a crown on the tower. Many a ship's crew inscribed their names in them; the most humble fisherman, up and down the coast, light up the night with the glint of sharp blades.

AMARGO: It's a beautiful thing!

HORSEMAN: Who can deny it?

(*The night grows as dark as a hundred-year-old wine. The fat serpent of the South opens its eyes before dawn, and inside the sleepers there is an infinite desire to throw oneself from the balcony, to the perverse magic of perfume and distance.*)

AMARGO: It seems that we've lost our way.

HORSEMAN (*stopping his horse*): Have we?

AMARGO: While we were talking.

HORSEMAN: Aren't those the lights of Granada?

AMARGO: I don't know. The world's a big place.

HORSEMAN: And so very alone.

AMARGO: As if wholly uninhabited.

JINETE: Tú lo estás diciendo.

AMARGO: ¡Me da una desesperanza! ¡Ay yayayay!

JINETE: Porque si llegas allí, ¿qué haces?

AMARGO: ¿Qué hago?

JINETE: Y si te estás en tu sitio, ¿para qué quieres estar?

AMARGO: ¿Para qué?

JINETE: Yo monto este caballo y vendo cuchillos, pero si no lo hiciera, ¿qué pasaría?

AMARGO: ¿Qué pasaría?

(Pausa)

JINETE: Estamos llegando a Granada.

AMARGO: ¿Es posible?

JINETE: Mira cómo relumbran los miradores.

AMARGO: La encuentro un poco cambia.

JINETE: Es que estás cansado.

AMARGO: Sí, ciertamente.

JINETE: Ahora no te negarás a montar conmigo.

HORSEMAN: You said it.

AMARGO: It makes me feel hopeless! Ay yayayay!

HORSEMAN: Because if you get there, what will you do?

AMARGO: What will I do?

HORSEMAN: And if you're where you belong, why would you stay there?

AMARGO: Why?

HORSEMAN: I ride my horse and sell knives. But if I didn't, what
would happen?

AMARGO: What would happen?

(*Pause*)

HORSEMAN: We're nearing Granada.

AMARGO: Is it possible?

HORSEMAN: Look how the balcony windows are shining.

AMARGO: I find it a little changed.

HORSEMAN: You're just tired.

AMARGO: Yes, absolutely.

HORSEMAN: Now you can't refuse to ride with me.

AMARGO: Espera un poco.

JINETE: ¡Vamos, sube! Sube de prisa. Es necesario llegar antes de
que amanezca... Y toma este cuchillo. ¡Te lo regalo!

AMARGO: ¡Ay yayayay!

(*El* jinete *ayuda al* Amargo. *Los dos emprenden el camino de
Granada. La sierra del fondo se cubre de cicutas y de ortigas.*)

AMARGO: Wait a bit.

HORSEMAN: Come on, jump up! Climb up fast. We've got to
                 get there before dawn. . . . And take this knife. I'll
                 give it to you!

AMARGO: Ay yayayay!

(*The* Horseman *helps* Amargo *up. The two of them set off toward
Granada. The Sierra, in the background, is covered with hemlock
and nettle.*)

CANCIÓN DE LA MADRE DEL AMARGO

Lo llevan puesto en mi sábana
mis adelfas y mi palma.

Día veintisiete de agosto
con un cuchillito de oro.

La cruz. ¡Y vamos andando!
Era moreno y amargo.

Vecinas, dadme una jarra
de azófar con limonada.

La cruz. No llorad ninguna.
El Amargo está en la luna.

9 de julio 1925

SONG OF AMARGO'S MOTHER

They carry him layed out upon my bedsheet,
upon my oleander and palm fronds.

On the twenty-seventh of August,
with a tiny, gold knife.

A cross. And so what!
He was so dark and so bitter.

Dear neighbors, bring me a tin
pitcher of lemonade.

A cross. Don't cry, any of you.
Amargo lives on the moon.

July 9, 1925

133

Attempting to Live Inside
Federico García Lorca's *Poema del cante jondo*
for a While

1

I'm convinced that some languages, languages we neither speak nor understand, are familiar to the ear. For myself, the Romance and Semitic languages, the languages of the Mediterranean and the Middle East are familiar to my ear, as opposed, let's say, to Slavic and Asian languages.

I come from a household of three languages—Ladino, Hebrew, and English—one that I could understand but not speak, one that I could sing but not understand, and one that is the language of my country, at some distance, always, from my own home.

So I understand Spanish, can speak it somewhat, and am still studying its nuances. I can read the poetry of Federico García Lorca in the original. And I was drawn to one particular book of his, *Poema del cante jondo / Poem of the Deep Song*, in part because I was drawn to the music it pays homage to, which also, strangely and surprisingly, was familiar to my ear. It resembled the incantatory medieval singing of the Sephardic synagogue that I grew up in.

The *Petenera*, in fact, evolved from Sephardic-Jewish synagogue song, and the Jews perfected its form. In "Description of the Petenera," Lorca dispenses with the narrative strategies of the songs, but the poems pay beautiful homage to the cry of their highly-charged metaphors.

Death travels down a road
crowned with withered orange blossoms.
Death sings and sings
a song
with her ancient white guitar...

Wind and dust
fashion prows of silver.

("Clamor")

I won't indulge myself here by recalling all the reasons why I
took on the project of translating *Poema del cante jondo*, or the
obstacles I encountered along the way. It is enough to say that
music itself became a constant companion. Lorca was a minstrel,
and he understood poetry as an oral expression. I found that in
order to come to terms with these spare, peculiar poems, I had
to come to terms with *cante jondo*, and especially the four *palos*
or genres of Lorca's book: "Poem of the Gypsy Siguiriya,"
"Poem of the Soleá," "Poem of the Saeta," and "Description of
the Petenera." Only by studying *cante jondo*, and translating lyrics
of songs that moved me, and listening to *cante jondo* while I
worked, did I begin to hear the strange, subtle rhythms and
silences and accents of the poems.

But I found myself listening to other music, as well. To other
forms of flamenco, for example; to medieval Arabic and Jewish
music; and to American jazz. I found myself going to the music
of *duende*, in other words, of which *cante jondo* is a supreme
example, including the American *duende* of Billie Holiday and
Cassandra Wilson, of Miles Davis and John Coltrane and Bill
Evans, of John Lee Hooker and Ramblin' Jack Elliott.

American *duende* was especially important to me during
those periods I spent living and working in Granada. There I was

thinking and speaking in Spanish. I slid into the ways of Andalusian culture, and it helped me to hear the language of the original poems. But listening to the music of American *duende*, music I've known and loved for years, helped me to hear my own language, the language of translation.

What is the language of this translation? It isn't anything without Granada, the Spanish language, English, music, the almost mythological life of García Lorca, and the elements of Deep Song.

2

In 1921, Federico García Lorca made a book of poems, to be titled *Poema del cante jondo*. He was twenty-three. It was his first mature work in the sense that the poems were not centered only on his own interior life. In fact they were not about him at all, but were inspired by a festival of *cante jondo* that he and the great Spanish composer, Manuel de Falla, were organizing. The festival would take place in 1922 in the Alhambra, and, like its ancient Moorish setting, would remind Andalusia and all of Spain of its deep musical soul.

Lorca referred to *cante jondo* as "a stammer, a wavering emission of the voice... [that] makes the tightly closed flowers of the semitones blossom into a thousand petals....

"Cante jondo... is the trilling of birds," he said, "the song of the rooster, and the music of forest and fountain.

"It is a very rare specimen of primitive song, the oldest in all Europe, and its notes carry the naked emotion of the first Oriental races."

Cante jondo is highly stylized singing. In each song the *cantaor* must convey his or her own suffering within the *compás* of its complex rhythms. And *compás* is a strange, unique fluidity—full of discrete interruptions, accents, and silences. In *Poem of the*

Deep Song, Lorca did not try to imitate the lyrics or music of *cante jondo*, but he did, I think, rely on its *compás* in order to craft poems that would enact the experience of the solitary anguish that is *cante jondo*.

> The wineglasses of dawn
> are broken.
> The cry of the guitar
> begins . . .
>
> ("The Guitar")

The cry is essential to *cante*. Not unlike the guitar, in fact, the voice of the *cantaor* is considered an instrument of the cry, the cry that dares to break the silence, just as the hands are an instrument to break the stillness, as are the feet.

THE CRY

> The ellipse of a cry
> echoes from mountain
> to mountain.
>
> From the olive trees
> a black rainbow
> veils the blue night.
>
> Ay!
>
> Like the bow of a viola
> the cry vibrates long strings
> of wind.

Ay!

(The cave dwellers'
oil lamps begin to appear.)

Ay!

3

Lorca loved *cante jondo*, and he believed it had to be preserved because only Gypsy music, the music of the persecuted and oppressed, truly embraced the richly diverse and ancient Andalusian culture that the Church, ruling monarchies and crass commercialism had so nearly destroyed. From Indian and Andalusian folk song, together with the song of the Arabs and Jews, Gypsies of Southern Spain developed and defined *cante jondo*, the song of Andalusia, and infused it with *duende*.

In a lecture that Lorca first delivered in Buenos Aires in 1933, he described *duende* as a "black sound":

> I have heard an old maestro of the guitar say, "The *duende* is not in the throat; the *duende* climbs up inside you, from the soles of the feet...."
>
> Spain is moved by the *duende*, for it is a country of ancient music and dance where the *duende* squeezes the lemons of dawn—a country of death. A country open to death....
>
> Everywhere else, death is an end. Death comes, and they draw the curtains. Not in Spain. In Spain they open them. Many Spaniards live indoors until the day they die and are taken out into the sunlight. A dead man in Spain is more alive as a dead man... [H]is profile wounds like the edge of a barber's razor.

Poem of the Deep Song did not appear in 1922, as Lorca intended. It was published ten years after it was begun, in 1931, in part because he abandoned it to work on a brilliant, even more traditional collection, *The Gypsy Ballads*, which was eventually to make Lorca hugely famous. *Deep Song*'s publication, then, occurred only five years before he returned to Granada for the last time, in the summer of 1936, to be part of his family's annual celebration of his and his father's saint's day. Four days after Lorca returned home, Francisco Franco, with the blessings of Hitler and Mussolini, initiated his famed rebellion from the Canary Islands. The Spanish Civil War had begun, and a month later, by then in hiding, Lorca was arrested. He was taken to the *barranco de Víznar*, to the hills northeast of Granada, and murdered. He was thirty-eight. And not until after Franco's death in 1975 were his writings or the details of his assassination openly discussed in Spain. Ever since Franco's death all the great *cante* singers of Spain have been turning Lorca poems into song. It has been my privilege to join them in their homage to the art of García Lorca.

—*Ralph Angel*

All quotations from Lorca's prose are taken from *Deep Song and Other Prose* (New Directions, New York, 1980), edited and translated by Christopher Maurer.

ACKNOWLEDGMENTS

Acknowledgment is made to the following publications for translations, some in bilingual format, which originally appeared in them:

The American Poetry Review: "Poem of the Soleá"/"Dry land...," "Village," "Dagger," "Crossroads," "Ay!," "Surprise," "Soleá," "Cave," "Encounter," "Dawn"

The Antioch Review: "Two Young Women"/"Lola," "Amparo"

LIT: "Scene of the Lieutenant Colonel of the Civil Guard," "Dialogue of Amargo the Bitter"

New England Review: "Poem of the Gypsy Siguiriya"/"Landscape," "The Guitar," "The Cry," "The Silence," "Siguiriya's Way," "After Passing," "And Then"

The New Republic: "Saeta," "The Way"

Ploughshares: "Flamenco Vignettes"/"Portrait of Silverio Franconetti," "Juan Breva," "Café Flamenco," "Lamentation of Death," "Exorcism," "Memento"

The Southern Review: "Ballad of Three Rivers"/"The river Guadalquivir...," "Description of the Petenera"/"Bell (Bass String)," "Road," "Six Strings," "Dance (In the Garden of the Petenera)," "Death of the Petenera," "Flourish," *De profundis,"* "Clamor"

"The Guitar" received the 2003 Willis Barnstone Poetry Translation Prize, and also appeared in *The Evansville Review*.

With many thanks to José Ruanco and Carmen Casado Gonzales for the friendship, comfort and context they provided during my stays in Granada. And to Greg Simon, for whose patience, guidance, and careful reading, I am especially grateful.

BIOGRAPHY

FEDERICO GARCÍA LORCA was born in Fuente Vaqueros, near the city of Granada, on June 5, 1898. One of Spain's most acclaimed poets and playwrights, he was also an accomplished artist and musician. As a young man, Lorca studied philosophy, literature, and law. He achieved prominence for his poetry in the 1920s with the publication of his works *Libra de poemas* (1921) and *Romancero gitano* (1928). Although Lorca wrote *Poema del cante jondo* in 1921, the collection was not published until 1931. Lorca's best-known volume of poetry, *Poet in New York*, which reflected his time in depression-era New York City, was published in 1940, after his death. At the onset of the Spanish Civil War, in August of 1936, the outspoken Lorca was arrested, executed without trial by Franco nationalists, and buried in an unmarked grave at the foot of the Sierra Nevada Mountains.